M000168675

Mass for Shut-Ins

Also by Todd Robinson

Note at Heart Rock

Mass for Shut-Ins

Poems

TODD ROBINSON

The Backwaters Press

© 2018 by Todd Robinson
All rights reserved.
Except for brief quotations in critical articles
or reviews, no part of this book may
be reproduced in any manner without prior
written permission from the publisher:

The Backwaters Press
1124 Pacific St. #8392
Omaha, NE 68108

402-452-4052

The Backwaters Press

Published 2018 by The Backwaters Press.

Robinson, Todd
Mass for shut-ins / Todd Robinson.
ISBN-10: 1-935218-48-4
ISBN-13: 978-1-935218-48-7
LCCN: 2018932775

Front cover: *Adios Esposito* © 1997 by Bill Hoover;
frame by Renee Ledesma

Back cover (author image):
The Toddfather © 2017 by Bart Vargas

Artworks used by permission of the artists.

Printed in the United States of America.
First Edition

for Cheryle, more than ever

Yesterday I wanted to
speak of it, that sense above
the others to me
important because all

that I know derives
from what it teaches me.

—Robert Creeley, "For Love"

CONTENTS

Mass for Shut-Ins

Skin

I want
to be less

of an animal
stop burying

my face
in her

pillow
& panting

the leavings
there—a soft

ravening
hominid torched

by rosewater
& coconut oil

Cento (found in the Midwest)

The palomino has opened up morning
in the tall grass west of the house,
among antiques and clutter.
Elizabeth takes her clothes off for the moon,
hoping to soak 1,000 miles behind the wheel out of her hips.

The buzzards circled and the sky was grey.
O lotus, daughter of the Sun,
I can't remember all the sins I should.
I'm never in my right mind for long, my wife says of me.

In the end
like shades ascending, this morning's fog—
small flakes still fell lightly
and yet we know the heart.

Why live here instead of there? Does it matter?
You with the gold tooth:
sounds in season decorate the starlit night.

Every summer I lived with my grandparents—
after a rain I yanked weeds in the flowerbed, crabgrass and foxtail.
Is it pathetic to see the insides outside?

All that summer they could hear the wolves.
If only we could touch like flowers bloom color.
Here's hard country to travel: even the willows
praise a day to do nothing.

We are in the Niobrara stretched out:
there are materials in this world that draw the body
into the blossoming essence of April.

The sky unrolls from the earth.
Late in the year a three-quarters moon.
I place flowers next to cold marble.
It is more comfortable than any seat.
Each morning, with the parting of the curtains, the world.

Postcards to Ourselves

What were you doing down by the *Vinca minor* raked by photons and hurt?
The neighbor's Pekingese were having heart attacks while we grubbed around
in the back fortieth, heat-waves wrinkling dirt. I told your father you were
the fairest daughter, but still he drank. Your mother kept her lump to herself.

Do you remember when we danced on a burning beach in those hills of sand?
Highway 2 felt like Mars, our crawl through to grandfather radio warble, the bend
of metal and rock, calf hair on wire, dry ponds winking as we worked our way
along the Pawnee trail toward reservations littered with plastic bags and satellite

dishes. Your little feet walked up and down my back, my hands held your fear.
Custer State Park, a thumbprint moon blurring our star party, my heart a trout
thrashing. Wyoming was the smudged aquarium glass of dream logic, the heat
of your cheek. Yes, the sky will swallow your blue skirt, my philosopher's arms.

In Missoula, we almost visited that little church. I wanted an offering plate
to hold campfire popcorn. You wanted incense to perfume those diesel clouds
and feedlots. We carved mold from hard cheese, slipped sardines down green
throats. The old man in the book store saying, *Take care, take care of beauty.*

Looking for Bill Kloefkorn

I thought I saw you amble
out from the corn crib,
counting fallen kernels
dropped in the years
of rusty cultivators.

How you did inhabit
those pitchers of sweet tea,
those half-lies of fathers,
white hair shining,
dizzy as a weathervane
through the last illness....

You climbed that hill
in May with a hospital gown,
a caesura blown
through the kitchen window,
the credo and benevolence

of Kansas in the trestles
of a tired rail town,
your seedlings covered
in alluvial loam,
sipping small rain
from the Lutheran sky.

Like a Mooncalf Under Plastic Chili Pepper Lights

Sigh my name as I churn within your cochlea, shudder the painted
    cave walls into nullity.
Loll fingers through my laughter, plant the cracked shadow
    of your lipstick on my chest.

Pour a pitcher of nostalgia into the grave grass while honey bees
    rebound and ripen.
Turn over the old earth, stir in the mulch of a thousand mornings,
    sketch the root-clench.

What were you thinking when you asked what I was thinking
    under the rotting trellis?
You should have known I missed you: the leather of your voice,
    the saffron of your hair.

You don't remember when we made love to Mass for Shut-Ins,
    the floor our cathedral.
We built tabernacles from dominos, hanging gardens of spent
    limes, colossi of matchsticks.

Where did you learn to shank me with a *bon mot* so, to rake me
    with those green nails?
You asked yourself to give every spare joule to love, or so you say
    you said, though you doubt.

On the 12th of September we drank many margaritas and mazed
    through a deserted mall.
I am told to keep this to myself, to bury the past in earth,
    in forgetting, in time's back forty.

Wind combs the bald roof, rain pelting like a bantamweight, all
     leaf-shine and power-line.
In the shudder of escape velocity, in the jumping children,
     in the cracked concrete: song.

Landscape, Still Life, Portrait

October here
with its golden
cold and nostalgia
cracking its weight
against my hips,
the black dog
of what I once
dared to say
tagging me
through shifting
grass, crows
worrying fence
posts, you
coming home,
your pillow
redolent of
something
greener than
your eyes.
I search for
a purple marker
in an empty
drawer. I want
to draw a daylily
on your back,
write *forgive me*
in Palatino,
scrawl a Ghazal
wherever you'll

have it, but
the marker is gone,
and my fingers
have forgotten
their Arabic.
The garage door
moans open.
Your feet call
my name up
the stairs,
another dress
whispers itself
to the floor.
I study your
vellum, words
forgotten,
the poem about
to happen.

Morning After Morning

after Steve Scafidi, after Ammianus

Moon after moon slides in its groove over the house.
Night with beer cans rattling in the foot wells.
Night with an owl. Night so big and blue with dark

to drink an eyeful is to swoon like a wastrel and sing
through the alleys. Moon after moon the bone plate
cracks to smaller shards until it evanesces into starlight

and bats all blunder home. The roar of God can be hard
to hear, the click of a casket lid or a silent film, the space
between a mother's birth and the last rattle of her last

child's child. A sphinx moth crawls upon a screen,
wings broad as leaves, slow to give up on getting in.
So easy to perceive all of this. Morning after morning

shakes off the dark and that bright glows everything
awake. By dusk blood begins to ache. Grackles titter,
clouds roil into ephemeral kingdoms. Moon after moon.

The White Pill

I took the white pill
this evening

I got new fuzz
on the bones

inside my skin
the missus

does her little sleep
on the sofa

and at dawn
a whistle summons

all the tiny workers
to their cubicles

it is silent piercing
not at all

like the shriek
of a failing republic

(Definitions of) Fun

1. If you piled all your coins on my belly, we could
have some fun. 2. Please let's not drive past another
feedlot. That kingly steer on the hillock does impress,
though, shit dribbling from under his tail like indifference.
3. One time I saw a neighbor and his daughter walking
and they hid from me behind a tree. I laughed at them,
though not with every part of myself. 4. Last week,
looking for beads to put in a piñata, I came across a
bottle of vodka, heat trapped in glass. I thought who
could I give this to? I was sober 360 days, a full circle
of recovery, but that potato sweat seemed too sweet
to waste. 5. Then I went looking for clay and found
a ball of hash. I remembered the times I had carved
shavings and burned them on hot knives, but I threw
it away. Forgive me, seekers. 6. We are born so cold,
but strangers swaddle us, wipe the goo from our mouths
so we can breathe. 7. My friend Kelli calls me weekly,
but I never answer, though I am often lonely. She is
beautiful, but we have never kissed. Her mother once
dated a helicopter pilot. 8. My mother once dated a
chef who refused to leave his ex-wife. I feel sorry for
all of them. 9. My father's final girlfriend died of brain
cancer five years ago. Suzanne, you resembled Billie
Jean King, which made no sense. Dads prefer blondes.
10. Another time my girl and I were walking under tree
shadows, a little high maybe, and this couple crawled

out of an argument, roaring down the street. We crouched
behind a car to listen. "Don't touch me," she said. "I will
smash your fucking face." We tittered, happy it wasn't
us, for once. She was blonde as ice. He was a generic
man, face rubbery with booze. Then they spotted us.
"Excuse me," she smiled. "We're just being vicious."

It Was Hard to Tell

We bought a vaguely representational statue of an antelope, elongated and yellow
with off-putting white eyes, for the little patch of yard by the mums. We talked
to it under a fingernail moon, told it why we married so late, had no children,
coddled our nieces and baked bland pies for the neighbors. We named it Grace,
then Hope, then Fidelity, then nothing. We let the next-door dog wake us

from dreams of hallways and mice so many times we finally snapped and flung
the bedroom window open, shouted Enough! I will fucking kill you and its owner
said Sorry I'm so sorry—Bob get your ass in here and we thought Bob a great
name for a dog. We mastered the margarita, perfected the fish taco, honed the art
of tchotchkes, found the best little Mexican grocery store, got drunk-but-not-too,

listened to crickets gossip and ignored reality television for a full decade while also
neglecting various local ordinances. We raked the leaves, we shoveled, we kept
the grass at heights appropriate to the seasons. We would have flown the Red Baron
kite her father bought us but were afraid not of power lines or trees but of a hard
landing, certain those plastic spars couldn't bear the weight of our caroms. Regret's

something you learn to ignore. We drank rivers. We listened to the rain from our little
porch, we hummed songs from our youth, we kept a tidy garage for a while after
we moved in, then surrendered to our clutter. We walked to a park, took in the rose
garden, the M.I.A. rock, the pine trees and clouds with their zeppelins and dragons.
We watched other people, their prosperity. We adapted to the aches suffusing our joints,

we played board games once a month, tops, we hunkered down before screens, lost
ourselves to the white noise of sprinklers and leaf blowers, the way silence never
really descended but when it did our ears rang so loud we had to turn on a song.
We wanted to shush our past selves. We were moving toward something, even as we
sat over our bowls of yogurt. We were growing smaller, or larger, it was hard to tell.

The Palace of Wisdom

All night the shaker rattled us awake,
two parts tequila, one part lime juice,

some Cointreau for sass and the odd
stumble underground for a spark to slow

time. Happy, we floated in a micro-climate
of chlorinated water, pink rafts and beach

balls bobbing with our moods, two women
curling in a hammock, elbows sticky,

laughter festering the air. Frank Ocean's
slow electric tongue lulled the after-party

nigh to heaven, immortality promised
in that creep of blackout's romance,

a last reveler bowing out the door
to barf himself half-sober on a patch

of drowsy hostas, sprinklers spitting
their *tsks* while the hostess, head kicked

at by castanets, groped brutal blinds,
groaning to keep some dark in.

Little Things I Know

Seventy percent chance of rain today—that's a free shower
for the dirty Kia across the street. Here's a dumb secret
I just figured out: everybody chose silver paint to escape
expensive car washes. It doesn't show dirt. That's the point.
Here's another little thing I know: there's a motherfucking dog
growling behind every sinner's chain-link fence, damaging

the grass because we're lonely monkeys. Life damages.
My wife says we're more apish than monkeys, showering
the porch planters with tap water. We've never had a dog
or a baby, because we're like that. I keep too many secrets,
have a hankering for booze, don't see any fucking point.
After work today we're going to get blitzed, escape

the echo chambers of our brainpans. Escaping
this gritty house is fun. It's all a little more damaged
when we come to, the knives in gray water more pointed,
the unfolded laundry, the ragged yard, the scummy shower
all we can see, but every house hides behind a secretive
door. Unleash the hounds of Saturday and get dogged

about spring cleaning, work like a serf until the last dogs
die and you can sleep in the quiet hum of clean escapism:
when your surfaces are spotless, you know the secret.
When I was a high-school malcontent I read a damaged
paperback edition of *Steppenwolf*. In the gym's showers
Germany gleamed in my eyes: a foyer, the rounded point

of a broom, a *hausfrau* engaging with her pointless
day: sweep and mop and scrub the world, tired as a dog
but proud as a parrot. I guess you can't say shower
and Germany in the same sentence anymore. Escaping
history isn't easy. But with a little brain damage,
self-administered, you'll forget, and learn new secrets.

I sit on this porch with my beer, my smoke, my secrets,
the missus going in and out the house like there's a point
to this or any afternoon. I just want to get damaged
and covet the neighbor's wife with the hot little dog,
tilt my neck to receive cold cans of American escape,
maybe get a little sunburned in the photon-shower.

I'd give my left tit for the secrets of a laughing dog's
bark or the way a pointer curbs some critter's escape—
the promise of damage. The warm blood showering.

Bricks of This Place

There she breathes
regardless of the affair,
enduring like a war
widow in May and keeping her
hand sweating in mine
as we strain to stay
when the last year has said only go,

yet I'll stalk home under 57th street
leaves and roll something mystical
to smoke—she'll just press
a cool cheek against mine
and wrinkle her nose
over to the neighbors to console
them over their dying dogs.

She reaches Underwood Avenue,
the dull cars, she
expected to eventually.
There she is
in the exhaust reading
the body language of joggers
and babies trying
not to breathe too deep
the toxic particulates—
she's so insistent.

Have we ever sensed
the shards of dull light
against the bricks
of this place and our ribs
straining to hold as gears
grind underground
in the air all over
and in our small talk?

Sounding Stones

I can still smell our first July, drunk
on a patio, Franklin's Tower burning
in Nebraska haze, tears of laughter
dripping onto our hamburgers
at the Blue Jay bar on 24th, absurd
hellhole where we learned to while
youth away a discus-throw
from the Joslyn and its Greek relics,
from the college where we studied
Hemingway in the gleam of Jesuitical
teeth, Omaha festering in weeds
and wasp-nests, just up the hill
from our first apartment where we
found the secret shapes of ourselves.
Baby, you make me crazy in this dark
park where we sway on a sculptor's
sounding stone, glory in this wild
green misdemeanor, the sculpture
on which we gyre (a little terrified)
under a margarita moon, salted rim
or opiate scrim; thank you for this,
and for your little fist enveloped
in mine on the dazed amble home,
veins drumming, July a paradise,
night snapping its fingers to the bass
cicada beat, winter but a figment,
our front door whisking us to sky.

Elegy for Summer

Childhood spun dizzy as a windmill
      on Uncle Don's tenant farm, where my country
cousins didn't have to teach me to slop hogs

or point a Daisy at any live thing drifting
      through sights slotted like a cattle chute.
Aunt Gay the diabetic poked fake teeth

through her grin, bared an upper hip to Don's
      slap and little needles, filled our guts with chow
and hymns while humidity ripened to bursting.

When storms rattled over the hills of chalk
      we leafed comics to cricket drone, whiled light
away, dragging plastic animals through stories

in a yard worn to dirt. Have days been as fertile
      since? In the chicken coop's muzzy dark,
in the river banked with ghosted cars,

the crackle and gawk of Main Street,
      the endless rows of corn and fractured
highway concrete, the old men listing

in coffin pews, night blacking the stained
      glass to a kind of grace, a painterly proof
it happened, that once we were real.

Daily Chant

Keep your hatred lean & direct
Don't ever switch the target to yourself
—John McKernan

You with the lazy eye
You and your yoga pants   stop bending over please
You with your ears crammed with sand
You in the thicket
You and your green eyes
You skinning deer   go away
You grinding the memory from your mouth
You with fingers roaming the keyboard
Hey you in the cloud car with smoke on your tongue
You Robinson
You too Gilgamesh and Väinömöinen and Lancelot
You Representative (R) and you General (Ret.) with fat-ass pensions
You and you and you and you and you and you too
You with the bindle burning in your pocket
You scanning the broiling parking lot with a hangover
No loitering   wait your turn
You with the bible on your desk
You who have yet to read a poem this year
You blowing leaves
You hitting snooze and spooning her
You with the chemo port
You drinking cava and you drinking wiper fluid
You in the ballet shoes
You polishing hospital floors

You on your ass in deepening snow
You folding origami aliens
You with the lump in your throat counting raindrops
You flying kites no tree can catch

You Will Be Held Accountable

As a child I believed in things: Whale-song. Astral Projection. MX missiles.
Christians. The margarine container said its own name. My father, scared,
hit me. My mother smoked endless Salems, pointing her eyes everywhere
but at him. I wish I could meet the man who invented the plastic substance
known as Nerf. It gave our whole block a reason to live. My friends lined up
on the lawn and I'd smash through them, then I'd line up and they'd smash
through me. Somebody always got hurt, but history taught us to expect it.
We also played Kill the Man, which entailed killing the man (with the Nerf).
Some kids called it Smear the Queer. Carbon-based bipedal life-forms
with names like Doug, Greg, and Bob, we had Corvettes on our t-shirts,
loved candy and war, though both hardened our arteries. We all evolved
into chunky adults, posing in sandy places, celebrating our offspring
and their middling successes. As for me, I have no children. I am a happily
married former junkie who eschews meat. Something else to brag about?
My wife and I once found ourselves blushing in a Vancouver elevator
with a boy, his mom, and Robin Williams. I wanted to thank him for Mork,
who made it possible for me in fourth grade to be weird, and to draw a poster
in which Mork mourned by a polluted stream, his hands balloon-like, crying.
I ached to speak, but elevators are awkward. It was quiet for a few floors
as his son, hair dyed several colors, wobbled like a little drunk. Robin loomed
behind him and said in a robotic voice, "You will be held accountable."
We exited giggling, the doors closed, and they rose toward their dark future.

A McDonald's in Nebraska

What thoughts I have of you tonight, Jim Daniels,
for I slapped the burgers down on the griddle with a headache,
sixteen and looking at the full future.
In my hungover fatigue, and scrounging for cheese, I stumbled
into the steel doored stand-in fridge, dreaming of your enumerations!
What buns and what braggadocio! Thirty cheeseburgers
and thirty fries! Whole families
waiting in line! Drive-thrus full of minivans! Apple pies
in their sleeves, hamburgers in their wrappers!—and you, Ronald McDonald,
what were you doing ordering a salad?

I saw you, Todd Robinson, hustling, a young, sweaty cook,
sneaking chicken McNuggets from the warming drawer and eyeing the counter
girls. I heard you asking questions of each: Who expedited
these fries? What price a McLean Deluxe? Is that you by the soda spigots,
Allen Ginsberg? I wandered in and out of the present and past
following you, and followed in my imagination by the Hamburglar.
We strolled through the kitchen together in our black masks
tasting Big Macs, possessing every frozen
delicacy, and never passing the cashier.

Where are we going, Mayor McCheese? The drive-thru closes
in an hour. Which way does your Billy club point tonight?
(I touch your buns and dream of our odyssey
in the cooler and feel absurd.)
Will we work all night closing this joint? The manager
is shady, goes out to drink, we'll both be bitter.

Will we toil unending for the new America of wage-slavery
flipping frozen discs of conglomerated cattle scraps forever?
Ah, dear short order cook, sweaty old pressure-teacher,
what America did you have when Ray Kroc first dreamed his franchises
and you got out on a smoke break and stood watching the future
appear in the gray concrete of another strip mall?

Reply of the Red Shirt

Answer this, female life forms:
a pectorally augmented Übermensch with frosted bangs
       and a growl like a cloud of Cuban cigar smoke
sidles up to you on the bridge, we all know
by the next stardate you are doing the cosmic
       Lambada
well enough to make a Klingon blush.

Because love truly does age
like Star Trek,
the early missions brawling through papier-mâché
       sound-stages like a love-drunk
lizard-man, Captain Kirk zipping up his boots
       in some star queen's quarters
after punking another tin-pot pretender,
       nameless you shuffling gray hallways to plastic chairs
for another plateful of gruel, maybe some 3-D chess
       with your annoyingly rational buddy.

Because it takes a chest-full of dilithium crystals
to power your heart past the black holes of the universe
of love. Notice: the red shirt kisses who? No one.

We, anonymous cannon-fodder,
we take the butt-end of the away-party's phalanx
and are driven mad by robot gypsies, telepathic rock-creatures,
the green-eyed radiance of a girl in Composition Class who seems
       way too smart to tango with a black-booted
clod like Todd.
It isn't logical,
but it is often true.

Galloping around the cosmos is a game
        for the young, so you must know her heart
is giving everything she's got to overtake
        your warp speed self-absorption,
which no tractor beam can grasp unless
you realize the sentient slime-molds and time pirates
            and that last lover of hers, the space hippie
with the blue lute you could never learn to play,
are not the obstacles to interstellar peace:
the only thing
stopping you
from being fully alive
is your fear
throbbing like a pulsar.

So hail her and say
let us boldly go, baby.
Set your phasers on stun;
that caveman with the foam club
and your own searing self-doubt
aren't worth a Tribble.
Beam up and engage engines,
finally ask her out
to explore
strange
new
worlds

and see
what happens
when the credits'
celestial zither
stops its wail

and the TV clicks off
to have her sitting there,
some star going
nova inside you.

A Friend of Bill's Takes Moral Inventory

At the House of No Hangovers, the bartender pours only coffee,
serenades me with the Isley Brothers every Sunday morning,
air-bass held high and funky, cooling me out for the sake of love.
So many stories and thought-lines in these rooms, the plate
of Christmas morning cocaine conjured again and again
for the sake of honesty, or that Bemis benefit where two patronesses
got in a bidding war over a macaroni-and-cheese-box swastika.

One was married to me, drunk on *Veuve Clicquot* while a vape
idled in my tuxedo pocket. Now we've got some forgetting to do.
Over another saltless dinner I think of vegetarian Hitler and his
flavorless meals. He loved dogs and mountain air, like everybody.
I shudder to ponder a thousand nights, tube blaring, head lolling,
glass of scotch empty as a habit. When I was a kid I ogled comic
books featuring super dogs in red capes, their red houses sturdy

on asteroids, waiting for a whistle only they could hear. Manhattans
were like that for me, the crash of amber on ice turning my bones
to jelly. I sometimes feel life is a Tijuana bible, each page a four-color
kaleidoscope of human folly. M. bought two hundred OxyContin
from his neighbor the widow. J. taught her little sister how to huff.
T. remodeled his heart, scar tissue filling those lonely chambers.
Next year will be summery as a clothesline full of winding sheets.

One speaker tells us she cannot bring herself to admit she's a drunk.
Another wants a face full of gunpowder to silence his keening.
My sponsor is so tender with cheer and rue I am afraid he will be
toppled by a passing Higgs boson. At the end of every session,
the same chant: *keep coming back, it works*. Everything is of course
nameless, forms an illusion, language that slips on rose petals.
I've already said that. At the next meeting I want to say it again.

Hard-Headed Mantra

Ice in my throat, ice on the road, sky rock-white and so far away perspective skews in a cold house, indifferent sky that makes me call Pops to relive the old rhetoric. When I was ten he stropped the prophecies that scored my bones forever: *for someone so smart you sure act dumb/space cadet/why don't you listen/bonzo/how can you respect yourself/fool.* I disagreed, but later sat so many nights, scotch eroding everything, stunted genius waking dawn after dawn to infomercial natter and a ballpeen hammer. Prophets are hard to trust, and from my woozy chair I can't say I love him or myself, though A.A. chips clang in a box. He wobbles through his duplex on a grand a month disability because some thug plugged him with a .38 in 1980, bar floor not quite Kingdom Come for the old man younger than I am now, though I was too bright with resentment to care much. Now I hold up an empty glass to the sun behind its veil of winter cloud-scrim and give thanks that he was spared to chastise and to help me move my shit from house to house to house. Two and some years past the last burn I feel the ice building back up. Snow muffles sound, raccoon tracks scrawl the yard, a perfect robin shivers its song—the city swims up from sleep to make more music. I am a nostalgic chump, want some tumbler of poison to make my machine parts hum. I am not unique in this, but still feel so urgent. I nod to the memory of smoke from my mouth, from the bullet-holed skull that mocked so well. We're still alive in our separate ways, both of us sober and bored.

Blueprint Blue

He caterwauled from a roof
deck, eschewed moon fever
and bats bouncing through
the dark, just like her.
Ominous tree shadows,
he thought, drumming
fingers on a parapet,
though the streetscape
was water-quiet. Down,
down through the dust
mote tumble of the house,
he figured good fortune
in tall ceilings, the spray
of gladiolas in a vase,
the way it all nodded,
Well played at the wishing
well. Cricket throb and a
blueprint blue pool through
the windows brought more
savor to the flagon of fire,
glass melt blurry to Chet's
embouchure, but something,
a new wheeze tottering
the reeds of his breath,
soured her sleep, sent them
drowning toward the corn silk
furze of a final hangover,
filaments silvering through
the grit of an inner river,
morning's vein-squall
dying down, down
to an infinitesimal echo.

Some Child's Wild Ride

The girl on the addiction show
has hair like a baby bird's
and everyone can see her
underwear when she falls down
all over the place in her wrinkled
skirt. The ugly sidewalk

pitches like the deck
of a ship on a Monday night
in Missoula, and the camera
crew is surely complicit
in my *schadenfreude*
a thousand miles south

of ground zero, easy chair
propped back, a handful
of popcorn uneaten, for once,
in my palm. She's a real
jewel-eyed weirdo, sort of
smart under all that mascara

and molly, goofy in the right
ways, artsy, fartsy, easy,
giggly, like my crazy cousin
from Kansas, who sells trees
to pizza delivery boys
and only does the hard stuff

on New Year's and Saturdays.
So I'm sitting here sixteen months
past my last dose, mouth dusted
with salt, my lady petting her iSlab
on the couch, wondering what's
right in a world where camera

crews tag along for some child's
wild ride while I want to wrap
her in a towel and drop her off
at the orphanage. Everyone cries
at the intervention in the shitty
hotel meeting room and I think

you poor little bird you have
broken a lot of fucking hearts
and I'm crying (just a little)
too and remembering
bowls and pills and bottles
I've poured into

my own emptiness
so when she agrees
to go to rehab
and gets on the plane
to tender music and jets
over clouds piled up

like marshmallows
and mushrooms
I have a surge of hope
and no longer want
to break another day's
light into rainbows

with mirrors and smoke
but the dark
on the television
at the windows
in my brain and everywhere
will always whisper—

An Agnostic Prays the Memorare

To you do I come, before you I stand, sinful and sorrowful.

Night rattles with dogs sulking over banishment
under powerlines thrumming from coal. The roof

makes a sound like a maraca shaken by a bearded
doomsayer far from Omaha where I eat ice cream

as an indulgence for my dinner salad. The devils
of the present and devils of the past straighten

their ties and scoff at my collection of paraphernalia
while those teachers with chalk in their hands write

the same word fifty thousand ways: *learn*. My mother
smokes her millionth cigarette on the other side of town,

thinking grace is the musculature of a cat. Those eyes,
blue as a robe, watching soap operas. Mary knows.

Her piety beckons from a bathtub creche, from lava
rock, from concrete. She blinks in dark. Yes, I am

nostalgic for booze. A bright wind comes over us
from Canada and the pines gossip like grandmothers.

Corner of Saint Cecilia and Rue

for D.B.

Alpha and Omega,
have I ever been as bad
as all that? The nickel bags,
the petty deceptions,
the morphine pills bluer
than sapphires tucked under my tongue,
the sin of mockery, the sin of self-pity,
the sin of oblivion?

Why do you exist or not
in an Omaha summer
just like any other,
the corner glittering with green
glass at St. Cecilia and Rue,
where memory sputters up
from the past like a hangover?

Why do my knees knock
when I shuffle-walk
into the Radial Café,
something besides hunger
clenching my innards?

What do I want, Cecilia?
A cup of coffee, bottomless and black.

Bill paid and regretting
one thing after another,
what is left behind wails
through the distance,
W. hollow-eyed
and haunted at the closed
cathedral doors, M. tucking
a twenty in the poor box,
K. chanting poems to heaven,

the old women bent
in their coffin pews,
the past miscarried
again and again.

Cecilia, how could I call this unbeautiful?
Could it be that hurt
is holier than happiness?

Now night
broils the windows into water,
house hot as a censer.
I pace the quiet rooms,
the after-scent of it all,
the far-off smell
of the future
in dusty corners.
But mostly motors hum,
as though consolation
droned in the grace
notes of sympathetic machines.

Lines Written on a Postcard of *Cristo Velato*

for Pete Miller

Slap it down like a toothache. All these fakers begging for numbness,
yet we all know a body zipped into itself, the itself collapsing invisibly
toward? Wake us to pre-dawn gloom with lampshade hangovers, some
translucent bell lowering itself—mazy arrangement of wires, blood wine
in a clay jar, a beatific retirement in the cloud condo. Given enough
breaths, you will go noir in the afternoon, nap to death, though nerve
endings may register the hard click of a casket lid. To paint sky blue,
I was taught, one must listen at the window, but apoptosis may undo
your patient ears and soon you will be plucking glass slivers from God's
clock face. When (oh when), my friend, shall we jettison the façade
of hospital gown surety to drink some slugs of real nepenthe?

Hell Is Other People

You make me feel sweet as nicotine, dreamgirl,
shivering on the early April roof, smoking clove
cigarettes and spitting clouds of castigation

at the sleeping sheeple below our sneakers.
There's something heavy and rancid and moist
in you that I love, baby-doll, and smoky kisses

taste better than taco bars and salad stations,
fresher than dusty lessons served up in cinderblock
classrooms. You make me feel lordly as a principal,

sweet-cheeks. Boundless swaths of brown
split-levels squat in every direction, citizens starting
to roll from morning driveways, AM radio stations

bleating, breakfast sausage decomposing in soft
burbling bellies as they wend toward their infinite
sheep pens, naïve dull plodding predictable chattel,

beneath our teenage scorn. All of this is ours, party girl—
sway with me a while, clove-smoke dizzy from the heart
of the geography of nowhere, king and queen of America.

A Cathedral in Nebraska

I'm not programmed to pray
but my arm-hairs bristle
in St. Cecilia's as they slide
a ten-spot into the poor box,
hug one another under
Rococo vaulting that makes me
nearly believe in mathematics.
Neck craned, I am proud of myself
for this gibe to faith, but I am not
so smart, pulverized my sarcastic
brain with booze and worse
for several decades, stared
and stared at television screens
with a lake of fire in my glass
while the world went wrong.
Yet for all that I stand here
in my sensible shoes, six months
sober in a cathedral in Nebraska.
I dip my fingers in holy water
and hold it, a thirty-year agnostic
having absurd epiphanies in cool
Catholic air, staring like a statue
at the stained-glass crucifixion,
lamentations of holy women
audible, saints up to their beards
with worry. Satellites turn and tumble
where heaven should be, reflecting
our faces back at us while the earth
warms like a disco floor. Last week,

I watched a widow at prayer,
wondered where and how she hurt.
Her little back bent over hands
clasped around a puddle of rosary
beads. How I wanted to go to her,
to murmur of the village where
yellow flowers once rained
from God's otherwise awful sky.

A Pocket Full of Nickels

Bill W.'s tenth call was answered
and so he was spared from the hotel
bar but my wife is more in love
with air conditioning and television
than ever before so why can't I be
cool and gritty if a drone can capture
my roof's hair-line fractures
and this hammock can hold my gut
burbling with gelato and a brain
stocked with memories of hotel bars
and hot-boxing cars as another pal
puts his dog to sleep but somehow
avoids divorce while oceans swell
like sickly omnivores and cottonwoods
fritter their seeds over the lawn
my middle age a reeling robot
who thought he was human until
milk bled from the suicide gash
screens screens glow everywhere
in our wonderful sober dystopia
I'm proud of you buddy she texted
from another floor *Happy Birthday!!!*
thanks hon I said with my thumbs
as sparrows thrummed in some puddle.

Nebraska City Psalter

Last night, sleepless and sore, I took
my body out into the dark with a belly
drunk with sobriety and walked.

Birds ruled the branches of a tired river
town, haze of August heat muddying
the starlight, chlorine glow of street

lamps and the jolt of coal trains
through the gut of steaming America.
Down to the river I rambled, bars

quiet as the houses of the dead,
trees shivering with secrets,
bugs bouncing off my forehead.

The place seemed ready to tip
and tumble into dirty water—
nostalgic ghosts keening in cabins,

calico dresses and work-shirts
quivering on the clotheslines
of the past. Westward, I turned

my sweating bones past flower
baskets and storefronts glassy
as caskets, the world dizzy

and dreaming me to the edge
of mind where I lay my searching
down to take in the canopy.

Slowly, the ink darkened over
quiet, hot, concrete, holding me
still, Job under the apple boughs,

rinsed by echoes too sweet
to tell, flashes scoring that heaven
so remote from summer purgatory.

Space garbage or cosmic rocks,
it mattered not the whole way home.
I slept, for once, like a happy stone.

Apropos of Leaves

We have to redefine God; He is not love at all.
He is longing.
—Thylias Moss

at last I saw him again
raking last year's leaves
in hot april he shuffled
pale into view and said

something about perspective
a tumbleweed in his hand
the small comfort he came
for which I burned to provide

I reached to shake his hand
and he hugged me which
he'd never done and now
when I float in bed toward

sleep my heart will throng
with memories
wind tugged at my little
stacks and I said the trash cans

looked like battered apostles
he laughed and said apropos
of leaves he'd almost died
in december the heredity

of his father's frailty
clapping hard on his shoulders
in post-op fog he relived
a visit to *cnoc mhuire*

where his great uncle
was one of fifteen irish
peasants who saw an apparition
of mary he himself had landed

a century later on the international runway
built to serve all those seekers
there are no fixed truths
I mused only an infinitude

of vantage points I never
liked religion or its tchotchkes,
the profane jowl by cheek
with the sacred he said

people buy their plastic
marys and go back to sacramento
or tbilisi and put them in special places
I have no gods in the old house

I serve with my rake
and my sober doubts though
I still bow to a hundred sins
offer alms in exchange for icons

but he didn't come to hear
my confession he came to hug
so we clasped again under spring's
eaves and said stay strong brother

and back we went to our separate
gethsemanes mother mary missing
but her teaching echoing against
concrete like the hush of brooms

At Last a Spray of Gladioli

in a glass vase,
the big yellow
doll house raided
by hornets.

She parks
her brain
in the coffin
pew and does not
flinch at hope.

Why do I
wince when
grace is said?

Who will hear
mother's
confession?

Our father
keeps at me,
his voice
bright with
contempt.

Mandala

monks wear sensible shoes
and why wouldn't they
chained to dying animals
just like the rest of us
charioteers
under meth-white skies
while channelized waters
brood under a bridge
named after bob kerrey
whom I happen to admire
very much though
when we met in a bland
kitchen he didn't seem
so magnetic

the bridge bobs us a bit
monks in sandals
and socks or beat-up
tennies chant and shake
bells the color of henna
over an effluviated
waterway with concrete
banks in september

dozens snap selfies
as these men
who have nothing
release it all
in the form

of a sachet
of colored sand
which ashes
its way down
to join the river
on the way to kansas city
and holy points beyond

they are fat or short
or mustachioed
like so many
spiritual beings
smiling then
waving goodbye

wait I ask one please
bless my friend
he is very sad

they can't know
how much he hates himself
but he gets a blessing
and pep-talk

when you are sad
everyone around
you is sad

people who live
in desert
see beauty

women in war
cut their breasts
to feed babies blood

they climb into a van
and float on radial tires
to cincinnati or somewhere
equally enlightened

while we are left
to roll back to
uncomfortable homes
in a comfortable car
with silence and memory
for once letting hope
do the talking
our sins sensibly forgiven
nothing in the mirror
but a river
of road unspooling
the future a bell
that won't stop ringing

Variable Weather

And the sound of the bugs waking up,
      chirping there. Yes.
The leaves, the leaves, the leaves

like the tousled coronas on old men's heads.
      Farmers, hunched over
kitchen tables, chewing. Adult world.

The tractors they pilot, farming
      time. Every John Deere
a kingdom, corn silk, pink light, the dusk

tattooed with grasshoppers, a drought
      or two ahead.
Roundup piss-yellow as it mists

the millionth row. The real work and sorrow.
      Buick on gravel fishtailing.
A thousand acres divided by five heirs

equals silence at the funeral. Stop
      speaking to your sister
forever. Call yourself godly nonetheless.

the incredible future

i
all students will carve
infinity symbols
on their desks
the world will buzz
and fester people
of all persuasions
will use their cell
phones solely
to write koans
which will staunch
the bleeding
of our race

ii
boneyards will seethe
with rain rain rain
the pentagon's
ten thousand drones
will take to the air
and moan like sad
hearted pet-shop dogs
before simultaneously
dropping their cargoes
of lotus blossoms

iii
each of the various
religious beliefs

of our planet keeps
us only partly moral
we want to sing backup
in some celestial choir
every day we pace
our to-do lists unable
to cross off a chore

iv
of laundry of grocery
stores of parents
becoming impossibly
wrinkled they are
the tricksters
of this story
for they will
disappear and we
will be unable
to find them
though we cry
and call and
promise at last
to be grateful

The Sparrow Has Trilled

into being among leaf
rot and blue trellis

south of the house, Japanese
maples in their shyest hue—

morning takes her legs
for a walk, hoping to ease
a night in the soil

from her hips, light watery
at the windows, night snoring.

August, the garden
a rusty tangle, our hope
for perfect plums gone.

Ice Cream Headache

Real nirvana in Grandmother's forgetting.
That farmstead with the shelterbelt run riot,
caravans of cars, all their chatter, drivers
humming, passengers' little games
of why didn't I leave there earlier,
any sunrise a new language to learn.
Real illusion, fire, suffering in
the withered barn. Corn crib rotting.
What do you think she feels in there?
Real spittle at the corner of her mouth,
real eczema, real head droop in the new
wheelchair, Delores and Margaret
also failing to rationalize their way
out. Reality pinches at the hip bone.
Real ice cream in the visitor's room,
real statue of Calvary, wingbacks
and dark drapes. Real buzzard.

Five-Mile Mantra

The marks left by something
    that has passed

shadowy Bison
on the edge
    of a dream—

we want to know
    the cloud-rack's
ragged bottom,

    trying
everything here,
      like a feather,
a voice.

Four horses
    keep running
    in the pasture.

Womb of sand,
    we love you
but long for rain.

I stand in the kitchen,
      cut crispy green
    chickweed,
taken captive by my own hands.

All summer,
I have been feeding
a raven.

It is a trickster
asking, *Are you afraid?*

The pond's dry eye,
calf hair on wire,

scent of algae—
green water still,
toes curled over the lip.

Potter's bowl.

Praise the Grandmothers

for their Astroturf porches and papery laughter welcoming you in.
Praise their Christmas-tree skirts and ceramic gnomes sleepy under
the azaleas. Praise their candy dishes twinkling like jewelry boxes.

Praise their kitchen bric-a-brac, their buttery breads and gooseberry
pies. Praise their costume jewelry, chunky as Betty Rubble's. Praise
their appliqué sweaters and goofy toilet-seat covers. Praise "We aim

to please. You aim too, please." Praise their silk flowers and faux
sparrows. Praise their doilies and tchotchkes, refrigerator magnets
cued to seasons. Praise their perms, refreshed every week. Praise

their plastic glasses and the pink lemonade therein. Praise canasta.
Praise their bird feeders and cardinal parties, their tidy bedrooms
and abridged novels. Praise their spider plants swaying in macramé

harnesses. Praise their pristine linoleum and immaculate garages,
their highballs and sugary spaghetti. Praise their ancient lips uttering
arcanities: "Jeepers! Oh my! Say!" Praise their ethnicity, scrubbed

nearly clean by America. Praise their men with craggy noses.
Praise their trips to all fifty states and the coupons they cut. Praise
their prayerful faith. Praise their soft hands holding on to yours,

eyes watery and weird. Praise their pastel pills in frilled paper cups.
Praise their soft forms under afghans sleeping. Praise the photos
of strangers smiling from nursing home walls. Praise the letting go.

The Giddy Centaur

I am a centaur
says the Facebook quiz
give me a kiss apple
break in my teeth
give me grassy kisses
I tell the hay bales
peppering Iowa
I canter a parking lot
and my halter falls off
it can't be stopped
the library approaches
it would like to shade me
but I am shivering already
my satchel is full of papers
not business papers
just piles of poems
I gallop past the library
with my four hooves
trampling the lawn
and become a rehab
joke: stay off the grass
I am so giddy
giggling always
easily persuaded
by a bare leg
there goes my mind
you are a dryad

I want to tell everyone
but my satchel is too full
everywhere I look
colts clatter
their hooves clatter

Up Through the Concrete

These poisoned sensations have to be
Accepted if they're to be
Overcome.
—Ariana Reines

The sway of summer light
from a woozy hammock
narrows to phone glow
and a recipe for vegan crab

cakes, not that I'll cook,
prefer carryout, let some
handsome immigrant feed me
drunken noodles with tofu,

drive past withered apartments
blasting holy reggae
to get my salt and fat,
remind myself the world's small,

same dumb moon rattling
overhead toward the pocket
of dawn, same potholes
chunking the car.

It was worse when I drank,
though it felt better to bomb
this noggin with beers and grin
past poverty's clotheslines,

little Thai girls in their ancient
t-shirts, mothers skinny
with worry. I've been ignoring
Portrait of the Alcoholic

on my bed-stand, desiccation
of the dry drunk. Tyranny
of laundry, tyranny of cooking
shows, tyranny of emails

cluttering my skull. Last night
I watched our feral leader
fail to crush a Frenchman's hand,
wondered when the other MOAB

would drop. "Without cruelty
there is no festival...." Sadism
of the long tie, the lizard eye.
Tonight we will practice marriage

by walking pollen-sick under
branches of bird-prattle,
her hopeful hand clutching mine,
clicking the day's rosary beads,

growing old as leaves
green and easy enough,
sacred and keen and sweating,
taking in all the light pollution,

forgetting the way home,
weeds fingering up
through concrete toward
all that pointless dark.

Renewing the Vows

My marriage is getting big and sex-addled: she swishes past me, naked
from the belly down, or closes herself into herself, television the only noise.
We drink margaritas too often, eat dinner in separate rooms, make amniotic

love in the pool, read Lorca aloud in bed at night, sulk and stare into dreams
we can never remember. She yells at me to turn down *Astral Weeks*. I beg
her to call her sister. She drops shoes everywhere, and I pick them up.

We put on pounds. We laugh at a comedian's bleak truths. We are inviolate,
spinning through St. Cecilia at noon, just us and two wiry widows in that cold
heaven. She slams the bedroom door. I stalk outside. She kisses my cheek.

We drink beer at a bar, conspiring to drive our crone of a neighbor insane.
She berates me for neglecting her plants. I belittle her in front of a dozen friends.
She tells me this is what I always do. I tell her she infantilizes me, buys me

underwear that is entirely too cute. We watch the *Lord of the Rings* trilogy
every Sunday in January. She orders endless textiles from catalogs. We
sway to reggae all through June. She hides from her family, from mine,

from everyone. I insult her for refusing to vote. She insults me for believing
it matters. We watch seahorses and dragons coalesce in clouds. She used to
believe in cloud-gazing. Our feet creak every morning. Our throats congeal

every night. Gray hairs begin to frame that doll-baby face. My back no longer
lets me take it for granted. Our mortgage is nearly paid. The lawn grows thick
and embarrassed. No one visits. We discuss the merits of quinoa, the verities

of booze, the infamy of Republicans. We drive to Hannibal, photograph
that tired river town, smell the musk of Clemens on every stone. She reads,
reads, reads. I fret about my teaching, and she says "I can't help you."

She tends patients all day while I walk the dog, graze Facebook, eat organics.
We shout. We chortle. We laze. We grunt. I ignore her calls from work. We drive
to Zesto twice in one day, sugar sticky on our lips. She refuses to eat Vietnamese.

I refuse to stop smoking. The house leaks. The hospital overbills us. We
assume old friends will never die. We used to cry together, but it's been
moons. Our bikes rust in the garage. We put on the Dead and boogie past

midnight. She gets buzzed and remembers her parents, gone now seven years.
We repeat our marriage vows, stare at the pictures of young strangers
in the big album. She rubs calamine lotion on my skin. I massage her shoulders.

She sings a song about her boobs. I make the bed. She offers me mushrooms.
I offer her bread. We fly to Kauai and Craig T. Nelson sits two tables away
and we say nothing. We kayak down a river, unable to build a rhythm.

She endures my snoring. I endure her negativity. We vow to stop drinking
for a week. We drink. I caress her face. She kisses me again and again and again.
We pick cherry tomatoes. She sews my shirt. I make her an appointment.

She tells me my mom is acting funny. She wants to know where I put her iPad.
I praise her toes. She tells me to shave. I put her green hat on a statue of Poseidon.
She asks me why I never write poems about her. I tell her every poem is about her.

Among the Octogenarians

Anything is enough if you know how poor you are.
—Larry Levis, "Sleeping Lioness"

Spring yawns a few weeks off,
sticks from the covers one cold foot.

Beneath ice dams
an old couple sits talking
about the renal clinic,
where no one, I think, is
looking at casket catalogs.

Maybe the whole hospital is dancing
naked. Maybe the old lovers dress
without wondering how
a body is dolled up for its unbirthday,
or how the Learjet
with those quiet golfers
kept flying until the fuel ran out,
while the dead dreamed of fairways.

A purple daylily is splaying
in a photo on my phone. I want
to splay and be purple,
and want only light,
the way a whittled cane
cannot remember the tree.
The phone vibrates or not
and means nothing.

I want to race forward and approach
myself at age eighty-two
and press that daylily into his hand
so he can see.
He will stand naked in a polished hallway,
suddenly awake among the many sleepers.

I want to be parallel;
the timeline of my life
never touching the dirt.

This Is a Good Day to Get Baked

I say to the blue clouds over the grocery store
where I just stocked my trunk with ice cream,

no booze. My sponsor believes in me,
but I have broken so many vows. Yesterday

I ticked past twenty-five months and thought,
you old fool you've done it or have you?

Now you push your knee into my back and sleep
just fine but how can I when I'm hanging on

that soft escarpment over piles of empty
notebooks? You've got to give me some space,

I say so low only ghosts can hear, and the lace
drapes glow like veiled saints against the night

with its same old moon and memories, the garden
listing into November. You look so tense, my love,

a furrow of concentration bothering rest though
your little body is warm and kind, susurrating

next to my no-sleep. You once sought God in the hills
of Dominica, danced the merengue at twenty-one

with a skull full of rum and the romance of the young
but that lecherous priest pushed his pelvis into you,

and grief was ground in. I think of this more
than is helpful. My desire is the frozen crater

lake of an asteroid, it threads an invisible line
between galaxies. I watch it from the telescope

you gave me, the expensive one with constellation-
finding software I am too hectic to understand.

All I see is the bend of darkness over the house.
We turn in bed like synchronized swimmers,

suspire somewhere in middle age. You will
dream of me, and I will dream of me.

"Cento (found in the Midwest)": A cento is a "patchwork" or mosaic of borrowed lines from other poets. The Greeks first created centos to pay tribute to Homer, the Romans to pay tribute to Virgil. This cento was created from the first lines of thirty-one poems in the Summer 2011 issue of *The Midwest Quarterly*. The poets are arranged by stanza lines:

Marilyn Dorf
Steve Nickel
Paul Dickey
Gene Fendt
Becky Faber

R.F. McEwen
Jack Loscutoff
Michael Skau
David Wyatt

Denise Banker
Susan Aizenberg
Clif Mason
Liz Kay

Cat Dixon
John McKernan
J.J. McKenna

Jim Reese
Twyla Hansen
James Cihlar

David Young
Janelle Masters
S.C. Hahn
Grace Bauer

Fredrick Zydek
Kelly Madigan
Neil Harrison

Heidi Hermanson
Art Homer
Dee Ritter
Ted Kooser
William Kloefkorn

"Daily Chant": Väinömöinen is a Finnish folk hero immortalized in the epic poem Kalevala.

"An Agnostic Prays the *Memorare*": The "*Memorare*" is a Roman Catholic prayer seeking the intercession of the Virgin Mary.

"Lines Written on a Postcard of *Cristo Velato*": Veiled Christ is a marble sculpture made by Guiseppe Sanmartino (1720-1793) and displayed in the Cappella Sansevero, Naples.

"Apropos of Leaves" is for Tom Prinz.

"Mandala" is for Firouzan Massoomi.

"Up Through the Concrete": The "MOAB," or "Mother of All Bombs," is a large-yield bomb first deployed during an April 13, 2017, airstrike against Islamic State in Afghanistan. "Without cruelty there is no festival" is from Friedrich Nietzsche's *On the Geneology of Morals*.

Many of these poems were ignited by the work of other writers.
I gratefully bow to the following forbears:

"An Agnostic Prays the *Memorare*": Pablo Medina

"Blueprint Blue": David Wyatt

"Daily Chant": John McKernan

"(Definitions of) Fun": Dean Young

"The Giddy Centaur": Heather Christle

"The Incredible Future": Matthew Zapruder

"Landscape, Still Life, Portrait": Drucilla Wall

"Looking for Bill Kloefkorn": Tyler Farrell

"Reply of the Red Shirt": Matt Mason

"The White Pill": Jim Carroll

ACKNOWLEDGEMENTS

Undying fealty to these friendly venues that have previously published my poems:

A Dozen Nothing: "The Giddy Centaur," "A Friend of Bill's Takes Moral Inventory," "Some Child's Wild Ride," "Ice Cream Headache," "Lines Written on a Postcard of *Cristo Velato*," and "Landscape, Still Life, Portrait"

All Along the Fence, published by Gibraltar Editions: "Among the Octogenarians"

Arc Poetry Magazine: "Like A Mooncalf Under Plastic Chili Pepper Lights"

burntdistrict: "The White Pill"

Canopic Jar: "Praise the Grandmothers"

Chiron Review: "Looking for Bill Kloefkorn"

Cortland Review: "The Sparrow Has Trilled"

great weather for MEDIA: "(Definitions of) Fun"

The History of a Day: "Little Things I Know"

Houseguest: "You Will Be Held Accountable"

The Journal of Compressed Creative Arts: "At Last a Spray of Gladioli"

Main Street Rag: "Variable Weather"

The New: "A McDonald's in Nebraska"

Sugar House Review: "Cento (found in the Midwest)," "Renewing the Vows," "This Is a Good Day to Get Baked," and "Mandala"

Superstition Review: "Hard-Headed Mantra"

Thistle Magazine: "Apropos of Leaves" and "Morning After Morning"

UNO Magazine: "Postcards to Ourselves"

Weber: "Nebraska City Psalter"

ABOUT THE AUTHOR

Born and educated on the concrete banks of the Missouri River in Omaha, Nebraska, Todd Robinson has spent nine months of every year of his conscious life in a classroom because nothing frees and inspires him quite like learning does. A proud graduate of Ralston Public Schools, Creighton University, and the University of Nebraska-Lincoln, he has taught college-level writing for twenty years, most of them at the University of Nebraska-Omaha. He has published work in such journals as *Sugar House Review*, *Prairie Schooner*, *The Cortland Review*, *Margie*, and *Chiron Review*, among many others. His first book of poems, *Note at Heart Rock*, was published by Main Street Rag in 2012. He lives in a crumbling manse with his wife, Cheryle, who left her native Sandhills to go to college.

And a giant group hug to the many as-yet-unnamed dreamboats who sailed with me into the dark sea of poetry: Michael Catherwood, Bill Hoover, Greg Kosmicki, David Wyatt, Pete Miller, Nano Taggart, Natalie Young, Maritza Estrada, Emily Borgmann, David Mullins, Rebeca Rotert, Sarah McKinstry-Brown, Jen Lambert, Liz Kay, Deirdre Evans, Paul Clark, Lindsey Baker, Ernst Niemann, Trilety Wade, Jennifer Robinson, Natasha Kessler-Rains, Genevieve Williams, Stuart Chittenden, Anna Monardo, Lisa Sandlin, Lisa Fay Coutley, Britny Cordera Doane, Michael Skau, Nicole Le Clerc, Bob Ericson, Brent Spencer, Paul Dickey, Robert Coleman, Grace Bauer, Ted Kooser, Marjorie Saiser, Rex Walton, Denise Banker, Liz Ahl, Michael Campbell, Nick Waggoner, Maya Pindyck, Millie Salisbury, and the Kimmel Harding Nelson Center for the Arts. I love you all awfully much!

CPSIA information can be obtained
at www.ICGtesting.com
Printed in the USA
LVHW111303301120
673019LV00007B/274

9 781935 218487